This book
belongs to:

Goodnight, Little Orcas

A COUNTING BOOK

Goodnight, Little Orcas

A COUNTING BOOK

by Megan Calderon
illustrated by Rachael Balsaitis

A&M Imagine Books • Chicago • USA

All inquiries or sales requests should be addressed to:

A&M Imagine Books
goodnightlittleorcas@gmail.com
www.goodnightlittleorcas.com

Printed and bound in the United States of America
First Edition
10 9 8 7 6 5 4 3 2 1
LCCN 2017941656
ISBN 978-0-692-88725-7

This book was expertly produced by Book Bridge Press
www.bookbridgepress.com

For my girls, Gabriela and Camila
—M. C.

To my dear S. P. and your infinite patience and humor
—R. B.

Evening is coming,
and it's almost time to sleep,
but first...

10 Ten little orcas
jump through the waves.
Orange-billed puffins scatter
under the last sun rays.

Then one little orca
drifts off to sleep,
floating, floating
in the ocean so deep.

9 **Nine little orcas**
chase sea otters around the bay.
It is their favorite game to play
at the end of the day.

Then one little orca drifts off to sleep,
floating, floating in the ocean so deep.

8 Eight little orcas
spot a walrus on the ice.
His long tusks and whiskers
make him look silly and nice.

Then one little orca drifts off to sleep,
floating, floating in the ocean so deep.

7 **Seven little orcas**
whistle a cheerful song.
A beluga hears the happy tune
and begins to sing along.

Then one little orca
drifts off to sleep,
floating, floating
in the ocean so deep.

Six little orcas
splash a boat with their tails.
The children giggle and wave
at the playful whales.

*Then one little orca
drifts off to sleep,
floating, floating
in the ocean so deep.*

5 **Five little orcas**
tease the seals darting around.
The seals speed away
without making a sound.

Then one little orca drifts off to sleep,
floating, floating
in the ocean so deep.

4 Four little orcas
glide close to the shore.
They notice a moose nibbling twigs,
and he looks hungry for more!

Then one little orca
drifts off to sleep,
floating, floating
in the ocean so deep.

3 Three little orcas
dive way down deep.
They see an eight-armed octopus
already asleep.

Then one little orca
drifts off to sleep,
floating, floating
in the ocean so deep.

2 **Two little orcas**
wave to the furry polar bear.
She plays with her cubs
in the frigid arctic air.

Then one little orca drifts off to sleep,
floating, floating
in the ocean so deep.

1 **One little orca**
swims toward the setting sun.
Another day is ending that was
full of friends and fun.

So the last little orca
drifts off to sleep,
floating with her pod
in the ocean so deep.

Now ten little orcas
huddle close and tight,
floating and dreaming
through the star-filled night.

Interesting Animal Facts

Orcas

Another name for orca is killer whale, but orcas are not whales. They are the largest member of the dolphin family. All dolphins are mammals. Mammals are animals that have hair or fur, breathe air, drink milk from their mothers, and are warm-blooded.

Orcas are very social animals and live in pods. They travel, hunt, and sleep in their pods. Orcas are found in all the oceans around the world, in both warm and cold waters. They communicate with other orcas using high-pitched whistles, clicks, and pulsed calls. Orcas are carnivores. This means they eat other animals. Their teeth can be up to three inches long. The white patch on their head can be mistaken for their eyes, but they have small eyes just in front of the white patch.

Puffins

Puffins are birds that spend most of their time at sea. They are carnivores. They mainly eat fish such as herring, hake, and sand eels. Their beaks change colors. In the winter the beaks are dull gray and in the spring they turn bright orange.

Sea Otters

Sea otters are mammals. They have the thickest fur of all mammals. When they hunt for food, they use tools like rocks to crack open shells. Sea otters sleep holding the paws of other otters so that they do not drift apart.

Walruses

Walruses are mammals. They spend half of their time on land and half in the water. They have two large ivory tusks, which are big teeth that they use for defense, cutting ice, and climbing out of the water. Walruses use their whiskers to help find shellfish.

Beluga Whales

Beluga whales are mammals. They are dark gray when they are born, and they can take up to eight years to turn completely white. They can swim backward and can turn their head up, down, and side to side. Belugas can dive underwater for up to twenty-five minutes before coming up to breathe air.

Seals

Seals are mammals. They have a layer of blubber, or very thick fat, under their skin to keep them warm. Their slick fur coat helps them glide through the water. Seals can stay underwater for up to two hours, and can even sleep underwater. Seals have whiskers that help them find food.

Moose

Moose are mammals. They are herbivores. This means they only eat plant foods. They eat shrubs, woody plants, aquatic vegetation, and buds of plants. Only males have antlers. They lose their antlers every winter and grow new ones in the spring. Moose use their sharp hooves and antlers for fighting off predators.

Octopuses

An octopus is a mollusk. A mollusk is an animal that does not have a spine. An octopus has eight legs, or tentacles. If it loses a tentacle, it can regenerate, or regrow a new one. Octopuses have two rows of suckers on their tentacles that help them grab things like food. Their mouths are located underneath their bodies. They have a sharp beak and toothed tongue to open the shells of crabs and clams that they eat. They make their homes in rocks or on coral. Octopuses have blue blood.

Polar Bears

Polar bears are mammals. They have rough paw pads to prevent slipping on the ice. Polar bears are great swimmers. They use their front paws to propel, or push, them through the water and back legs to steer. They have a strong sense of smell to detect seals, their main food source.

For activities and additional information about orcas and other arctic animals, visit these great websites:

Animal Facts for Kids/Animal Coloring Pages
www.animalfactguide.com

National Geographic Kids
http://kids.nationalgeographic.com/animals

National Wildlife Federation
www.nwf.org

Orca Habitat Map

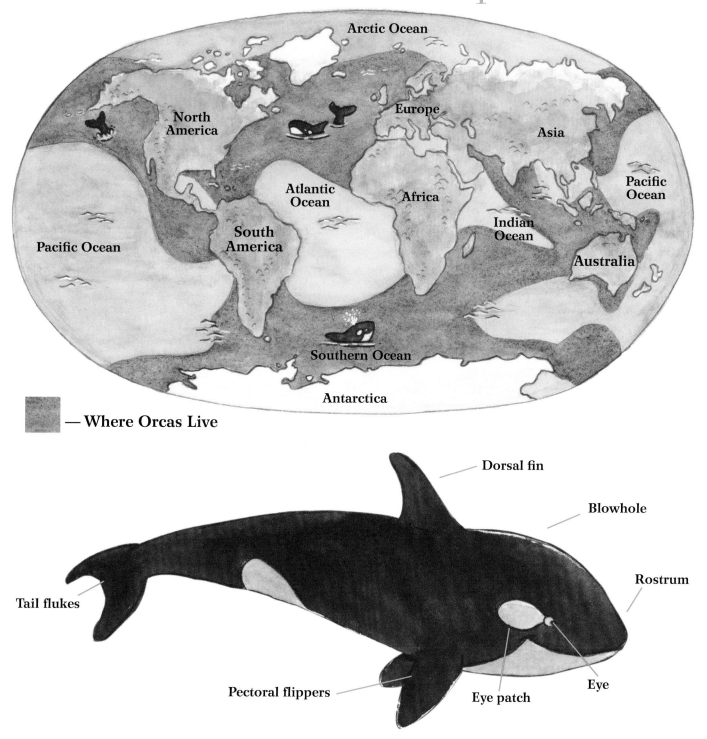

Arctic Ocean

North America

Europe

Asia

Pacific Ocean

Atlantic Ocean

Africa

Pacific Ocean

South America

Indian Ocean

Australia

Southern Ocean

Antarctica

— Where Orcas Live

Dorsal fin

Blowhole

Rostrum

Tail flukes

Pectoral flippers

Eye patch

Eye

MEGAN CALDERON grew up in Troy, Michigan,
and now lives in Chicago with her husband Alejandro
and their two daughters, Gabriela and Camila.
Goodnight, Little Orcas was inspired by her daughter's love
of stuffed animals and books. Megan wanted Gabriela
to have a fun book featuring orcas
to go along with her favorite stuffed orca.

Megan is a Chicago Public Schools first-grade teacher
in the Little Village neighborhood.
Her hope is that *Goodnight, Little Orcas* will spark children's
interest in ocean animals and marine life.

RACHAEL BALSAITIS is a Twin Cities illustrator
with a soft spot for all things quirky.
When not drawing, she can be found reading the Sunday funnies,
walking along the lakeshore,
or laughing at British comedies.